Read-About® Holidays

Halloween

By David F. Marx

Consultant
Katharine A. Kane, Reading Specialist
Former Language Arts Coordinator
San Diego County Office of Education

Children's Press®
A Division of Grolier Publishing
New York   London   Hong Kong   Sydney
Danbury, Connecticut

Visit Children's Press® on the Internet at:
http://publishing.grolier.com

Designer: Herman Adler Design Group
Photo Researcher: Caroline Anderson

Library of Congress Cataloging-in-Publication Data

Marx, David F.
    Halloween / by David F. Marx.
      p. cm. — (Rookie read-about holidays)
      Includes index.
      ISBN 0-516-22206-6 (lib. bdg.)   0-516-27154-7 (pbk.)
      1. Halloween—Juvenile literature. [1. Halloween. 2. Holidays.] I. Title.
    GT4965.M26   2000
    394.2646—dc21
                                       00-022631

GROLIER
PUBLISHING

Do you celebrate Halloween?

Halloween is a very old holiday. It began hundreds of years ago in countries in Europe.

Celebrating Halloween long ago

Back then, some people believed that ghosts came out at night on October 31.

That is still the date we celebrate Halloween.

Not many people believe
in ghosts today. But we
do think it is fun to dress
up as ghosts . . .

9

. . . and monsters, and witches, and aliens.

Some kids think it is fun to wear scary costumes.

Other children do
not like scary things.

You can dress up as
anything you want
to be on Halloween.

13

Most people like to
carve faces on pumpkins
for Halloween.

Put a candle inside, and you have a jack-o'-lantern.

When you carve
your pumpkin, do not
throw away the seeds!

Pumpkin seeds can be
toasted. You can eat
them as a snack.

Pumpkin seeds

At Halloween parties, some kids like to bob for apples.

They use their teeth to grab a floating apple from a tub of water. No hands allowed!

Trick-or-treating is one of the best parts of Halloween.

When you go trick-or-treating, it is important to be safe.

Always go trick-or-treating
with an adult.

Your costume should
be made of bright, shiny
colors so you can be seen
in the dark.

Be sure to bring a flashlight!

The best time to go
trick-or-treating is during
the day. It is just as fun
as going at night.

Besides, you can see all
your friends' costumes
in the light!

Do not eat any treats until you get home.

Your parents need to look at all your candy to make sure everything is safe.

Now you can enjoy
your treats!

While you eat your
Halloween candy,
you can start thinking
about a very important
question. . .

What will you dress
up as *next year?*

Words You Know

bobbing for apples

carve

costumes

jack-o'-lantern

pumpkin seeds

trick-or-treating

31

Index

About the Author

David F. Marx is an author and editor of children's books.
He resides in the Chicago area.

Photo Credits

Photographs ©: Corbis-Bettmann: 23 (Jeffry W. Myers), 5; Liaison Agency, Inc.:
10 (Robert C. Burke); PhotoEdit: 28 (Amy C. Etra), 27 (Michael Newman),
17, 31 bottom left (David Young-Wolff); Stock Boston: 14, 30 bottom left
(Laima Druskis), 20, 31 right (Charles Gupton), 19, 30 top (Mary E. Messenger),
24 (Jeff Persons); Superstock, Inc.: 6, 15, 31 top left; Tony Stone Images: 13, 30
bottom right (Kate Connell), 9 (David J. Sams), cover, 3 (David Young-Wolff).